Preschool — Alphabet, Colors, Numbers, Shapes

Activities for Building Core Knowledge

Written by
Mary Tucker,
Kim Rankin,
Karen Scanlon
and Lily Erlic

Illustrated by
Veronica Terrill and
Vanessa Countryman

Teaching & Learning Company
1204 Buchanan St., P.O. Box 10
Carthage, IL 62321-0010

This book belongs to

_____

Table of Contents

Alphabet 3

Colors 28

Numbers 53

Shapes 75

Cover design by Jenny Morgan and Sara King.

Copyright © 2007, Teaching & Learning Company

ISBN 13: 978-1-57310-527-9

ISBN 10: 1-57310-527-9

Printing No. 987654321

**Teaching & Learning Company
1204 Buchanan St., P.O. Box 10
Carthage, IL 62321-0010**

Several of the activities in this book involve preparing, tasting and sharing food items. We urge you to be aware of any food allergies or restrictions your students may have and to supervise these activities diligently. All food-related suggestions are identified with this allergy-alert symbol: ⚠

Please note: Small food items (candies, raisins, cereal, etc.) can also pose a choking hazard.

At the time of publication, every effort was made to insure the accuracy of the information included in this book. However, we cannot guarantee that the agencies and organizations mentioned will continue to operate or to maintain these current locations.

The purchase of this book entitles teachers to make copies for use in their individual classrooms only. This book, or any part of it, may not be reproduced in any form for any other purposes without prior written permission from the Teaching & Learning Company. It is strictly prohibited to reproduce any part of this book for an entire school or school district, or for commercial resale. The above permission is exclusive of the cover art, which may not be reproduced.

All rights reserved. Printed in the United States of America.

Activities

Alphabet

Letter Review

After introducing a series of letters, try this activity. List the letters you want children to review (four to eight letters work well). Have children write each letter on a large scrap of paper. Ask the class a question such as "What letter sound do you hear at the beginning of the word *apple*?" Have children respond by holding up one of their letters.

Letter Posters

Have children look through magazines and cut out letters. To make ABC posters, have them glue their letters on a sheet of poster board in alphabetical order.

Midnight Letters

Have children sit close together, then darken the room. Hand a flashlight to one child. Let the child "write" a letter on the ceiling using the flashlight. Let the other children try to guess the letter. After the letter has been guessed, the flashlight should be passed to another child. Continue until all children have had a chance to play.

Short Vowel Flowers

Use the patterns on page 5 to show different vowel sounds. Call out a "short a" word that uses the letters, such as *cat*. Go through all the words on each flower. Take children outside to use sidewalk chalk on the pavement to make flower vowel words.

Hop and Spell

This fun game encourages thinking and letter recognition. Write letters of the alphabet that you have been studying on separate sheets of paper. Place the letters close together on the floor in random order. Ask a child to hop on a letter and then think of a word that begins with that letter. If correct, the child hops on the next letter and thinks of a matching word and so on.

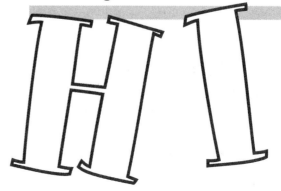

Colorful Place Mats and Place Cards

Reproduce the clip art letters on pages 25-26 and let children make place mats. Have them decorate 9" x 12" sheets of paper with the letters and creative designs.

For place cards, instruct children to fold 3" x 5" index cards in half. Cut out a letter from the clip art pages that is the beginning letter of their name. Glue it on the card. Then have children finish writing their names.

ABC Magnets

Cut letters from craft foam sheets and place a magnet on the back of each. On a magnetic board, help children spell simple three-letter words.

(These letters also work great for bulletin boards and are durable.)

Short Vowel Flowers

Bulletin Board

Alphabet

1. Cover a bulletin board with plain paper that may be written on.
2. Cut out the letters for the caption "Starring the Letter" and mount them at the top of the board.
3. Each week, enlarge and cut out a different alphabet letter. Mount the letter in a construction paper, star-shaped frame (pattern on page 7) at the center of the board.
4. Ask children with names that begin with that letter to stand or raise their hands. Print their names on the board. Ask if any months of the year or days of the week start with that letter. Print them on the board.
5. During the week, have children think about and listen for words that start with that letter. Print these words on the board as shown.
6. Have children look through magazines, gardening catalogs and other printed materials to find and cut out pictures of things, people, animals and words that start with that letter. Let them attach the pictures and words to the board.
7. When the week is over, start a new bulletin board with the same caption but a different background.

Alphabet Books

Alphabet Adventure
Written by Audrey Wood
Illustrated by Bruce Wood
Blue Sky Press, 2001

Charley's alphabet has been working hard all summer on Alphabet Island, getting ready for the first day of school. When their teacher lines up all the lowercase letters they discover that the "i" lost its dot. Children will love following the mystery and will meet the capital letters along the way as well. *Alphabet Adventure* is a terrific teaching tool and an engaging way for children to begin recognizing letters and learning phonics.

Alphabet Under Construction
Written and Illustrated by Denise Fleming
Henry Holt & Co., 2002

This book is a real find as it follows a mouse hard at work, constructing the letters of the alphabet. For example, he airbrushes an *A*, levels an *L* and measures an *M*. The bold, vibrant artwork dazzles with entertaining details and engaging humor. This is not an ordinary alphabet book—it is an imaginative, inventive, joyous romp that should not be missed.

Chicka Chicka Boom Boom
Written by Bill Martin, Jr.
and John Archambault
Illustrated by Lois Ehlert
Simon & Schuster, 1989

This book is a definite must-have for every classroom and household. Children as young as two years of age can learn the alphabet with the perfectly-timed text and vibrant illustrations. Kids will want to read this book over and over and will remember the verses for years to come. An absolute delight!

Dr. Seuss's ABC's
Written by Dr. Seuss
Random House Books, 1960

The entire book is one memorable verse after another paired with equally memorable illustrations. Typical of all Dr. Seuss books, the meter of the rhymes is fantastic, and the alliterations make this one of the best alphabet books available. Dr. Seuss makes learning the alphabet fun!

Peanut Butter & Jellyfishes: A Very Silly Alphabet Book
Written by Brian P. Cleary
Illustrated by Betsy E. Snyder
Millbrook Press, 2006

This will be a new favorite in anyone's collection of alphabet books. The rhymes are cute and clever, and the book is beautifully illustrated. Young children will love looking at all of the details in the pictures and will especially enjoy looking for the hidden letter on each page.

Crafts

Alphabet

Alphabet Review Pocket

Materials
- 2 paper plates
- crayons or colored markers
- yarn
- tape
- hole punch
- glue
- scissors
- ABC cards

Directions

1. Give each child a paper plate to color.
2. Cut a second paper plate in half. Have each child print on the back of the half plate *My ABCs* along with his or her name. Then let them decorate the half plate.
3. Help children glue the half plate to the whole plate by spreading glue just around the rim. (The two plates should be front to front.)
4. When the glue is dry, punch holes evenly around the glued rims of the plates.
5. Beginning on one side, have children lace or "sew" yarn through the holes, tying a knot at each end. (To make the yarn easier to poke through the holes, wrap tape around one end.)
6. Give each child a copy of the ABC cards (page 10). (You may want to copy the page on tagboard to make the cards sturdier, and laminate them so the cards can be used over and over.) Have children cut the ABC cards apart, or do it for them.
7. Let them put the cards in their paper plate pockets. Explain that they can take the cards out whenever they want to practice the alphabet by putting the cards in alphabetical order on their desks.

ABC Cards

Aa	Bb	Cc	Dd
Ee	Ff	Gg	Hh
I i	Jj	Kk	Ll
Mm	Nn	Oo	Pp
Qq	Rr	Ss	Tt
Uu	Vv	Ww	Xx
	Yy	Zz	

Poems

Alphabet

An Alphabet Poem

I like to say the alphabet.
I like to print each letter,
And putting them together
Into words is even better.
I'm proud I know my ABCs.
I learned them all at school.
Listen as I say them
'Cause I think they're really cool!
A-B-C-D-E-F-G,
H-I-J-K-L,
M-N-O-P-Q-R-S—
Can't I say them well?
T-U-V-W
X and Y and Z.
That's the end. Now aren't you proud
Of A-B-C-D Me?

by Mary Tucker

Alphabet ACTION RHYMES

Alphabet Song

Children will enjoy singing this lively song, but they'll need to say the letters of the fourth line quickly to get them all in.

To the tune of "When Johnny Comes Marching Home Again" or "The Ants Go Marching One by One."

If you want to learn the alphabet today, today,
Sing the letters in a song, yes that's the way
A B C D E F G,
H I J K L M N O P,
Q R S T U V,
W X Y Z!

by Mary Tucker

Alphabet ACTION RHYMES

ABCs Action Rhyme

As children say this rhyme, have them touch their fingers, toes, ears, eyes, nose and mouth at the appropriate times.

I only have 10 fingers
   (Wiggle all your fingers.)
And 10 tiny, little toes.
   (Wiggle your toes.)
That's not enough to count my ABCs on,
   (Shake your head no.)
I suppose.
I'll have to add my ears
   (Point to your ears.)
And my nose and mouth and eyes
   (Point to these.)
To make up 26 touchpoints
   (Touch your fingers together.)
For an ABC surprise!
   (Smack your hands together and out.)
My fingers: A-B-C-D-E,
   (Count these letters on your fingers.)
F-G-H-I and J.
My toes: K-L-M-N-O-P,
   (Count these letters on your toes.)
Q-R-S-T—Hooray!
My ears are letters U and V.
   (Touch each ear.)
My nose is W.
   (Touch your nose.)
I touch my eyes for X and Y,
   (Touch each eye.)
My mouth is Z. I'm through!
   (Touch your mouth; then hold your hands over your head.)

by Mary Tucker

Snacks

Alphabet

Writing with Pudding

Children will discover that learning the alphabet can be fun and delicious!

Make instant pudding according to directions. Add 1 tablespoon cornstarch and mix well. Have children wash their hands. Place a sheet of waxed paper in front of each child. Give each child a bowl of pudding. Have them dip their fingers in the pudding and spread it on the waxed paper. Call out letters and have children practice writing them.

Alphabet Bread

Have children wash their hands. Give each child one or two refrigerator biscuits to roll in long ropes and then shape into letters. Place the letters on cookie sheets. Brush them with butter, and sprinkle with cinnamon and sugar. Bake according to the biscuit directions.

Alphabet Soup

In a slow cooker, combine 1 can beef broth, 1 can stewed tomatoes, 1 can tomato juice, 1 packet dried vegetable soup. Add 1 package frozen mixed vegetables and 1 package alphabet noodles. Let simmer for several hours. Serve with crackers, cheese and apple slices.

⚠ Make sure you are aware of any food allergies or restrictions students may have. Be sure children wash their hands and the apples before they eat.

My Alphabet Book

_____
Name

A is for apple.

B is for ball.

C is for car.

D is for doll.

 E is for elephant.

 F is for frog.

 G is for gorilla.

 H is for hog.

2

I is for ice cream.

J is for jam.

K is for kitten.

L is for lamb.

3

15

M is for mother.

N is for nail.

O is for octopus.

P is for pail.

4

Q is for queen.

R is for rose.

S is for sun.

T is for toes.

5

16

TLC10527 Copyright © Teaching & Learning Company, Carthage, IL 62321-0010

U is for umbrella.

V is for vase.

W is for water

I splash on my face.

X is for X-ray.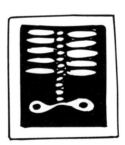

Y is for you.

Z is for zebra

Who lives at the zoo.

Name

From A to Z

Have letter A follow the path that leads to letter Z.

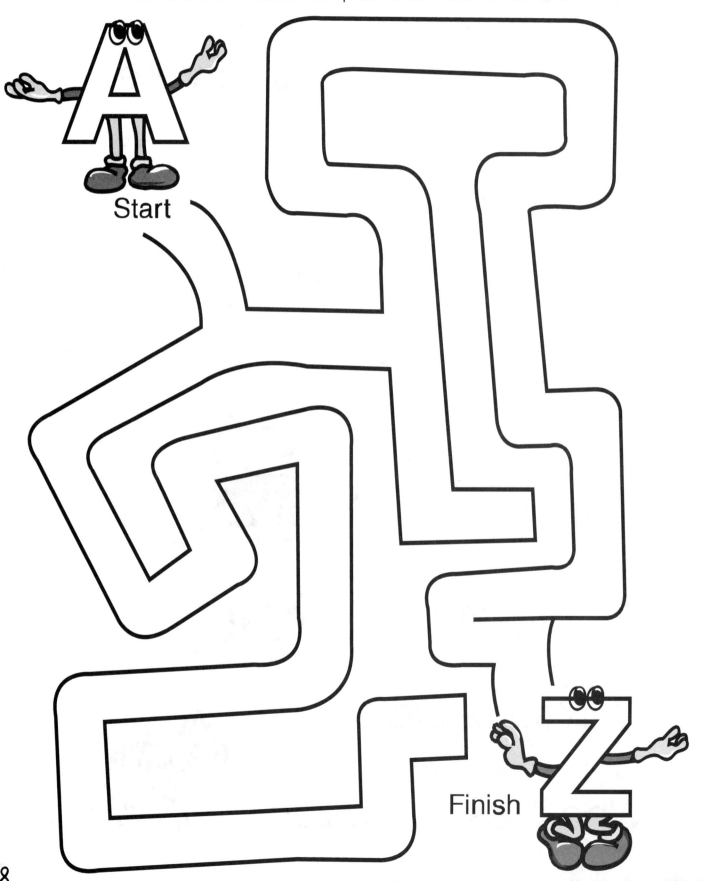

Start

Finish

Name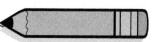

Guess Who?

Connect the dots from A to Z. Then color the picture.

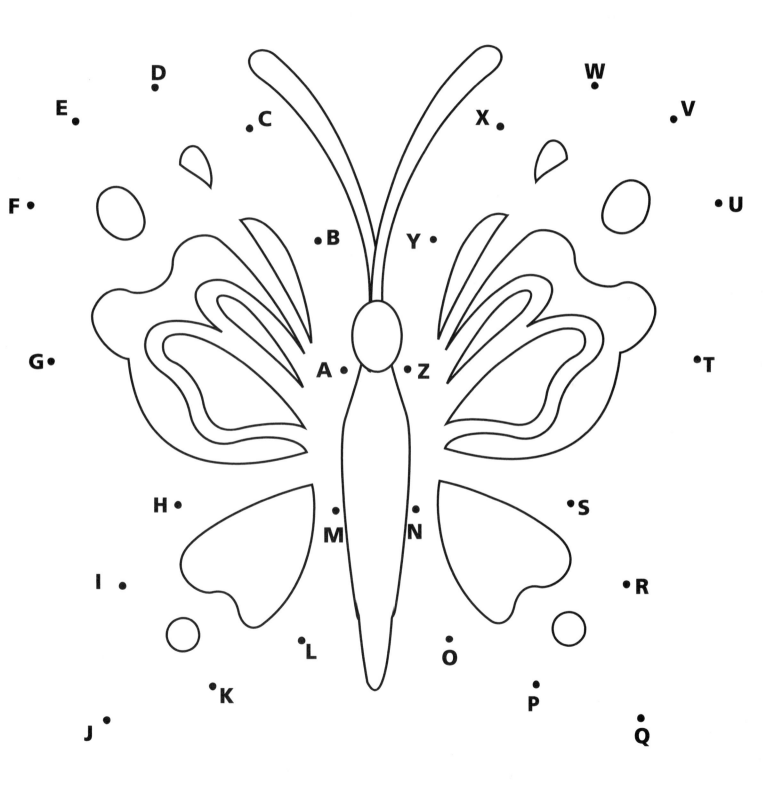

What Comes Next?

Beginning with letter A, follow the letters in alphabetical order.
Draw one line from A to Z.

C D E A F J W I E J L A
N W B Q J O M P S E C M
Q O C D A X I C E N S O
E A L P E F L X R W A K
I M V B D W G H I D V B
Y E P A D U Q Z J K L C
K D R G B N C X K L M N
O K X S E R T L B P O S
T U R S E Q L R Q Y Z A
S C U G U T S N L S P C
A O W V Q M B C P R W Q
C D X Y Z L N M H S C Z

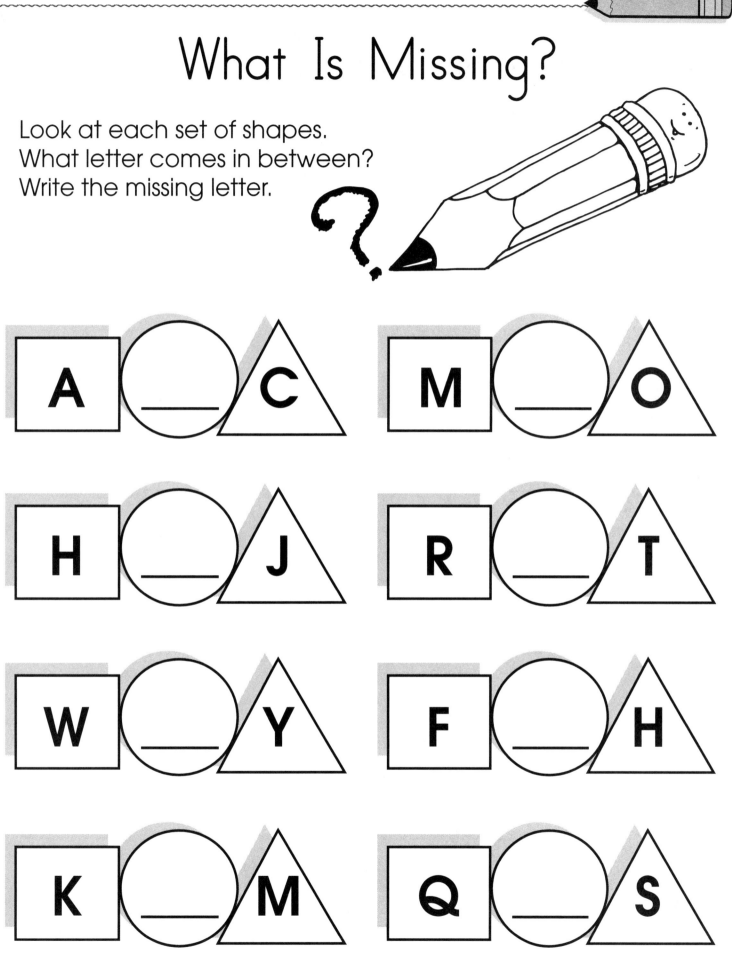

Name

Capital Letter Writing

Can you write the alphabet? Trace each letter. Say each letter by name. On the lines at the bottom, print your name in capital letters.

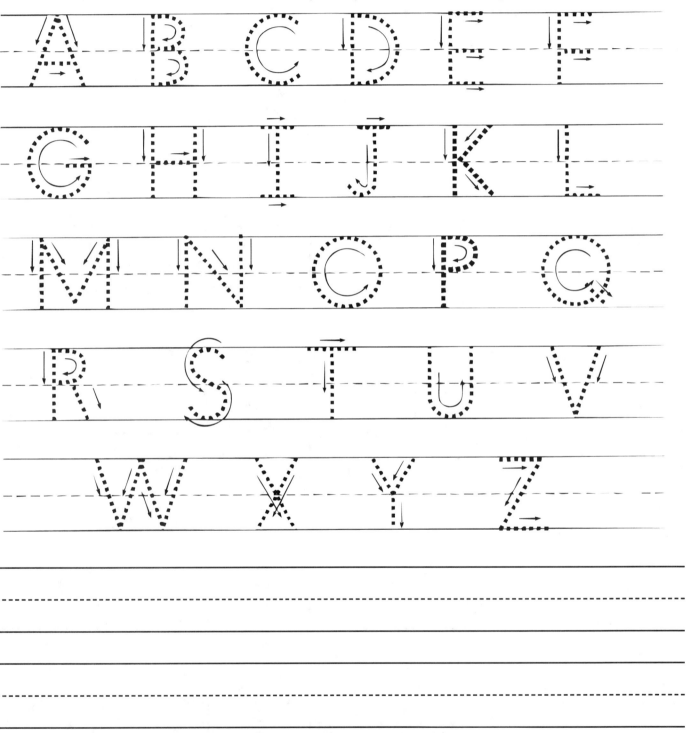

Name

Lowercase Letter Writing

Can you write the alphabet? Trace each letter. Say each letter by name.
On the lines at the bottom, print your name in lowercase letters.

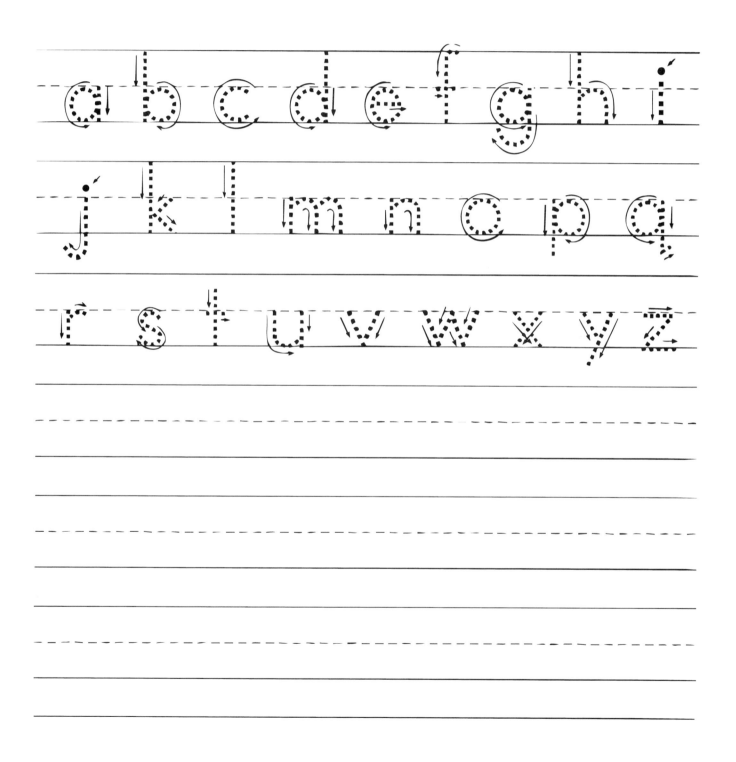

Name _____

My ABC Page

Clip Art

Activities

Colors

Can You Make a Rainbow?

Water is colorless and takes on whatever coloring is added. Fill several clear glasses with water. Add a drop of blue food coloring to one of the glasses. In another glass, add red food coloring. In a third glass add yellow. These are the primary colors. What colors do you get when you mix blue and red, red and yellow, or blue and yellow? These will make the secondary colors (purple, orange, green). Demonstrate with the glasses of water.

Color Hunt

Divide the class into several small groups. Each group needs a bag with a different color tag attached to it. Each group will search the classroom, collecting three to five items that match the tag color on their bag. Have the groups share their findings.

Color Beanbag Toss

You will need several beanbags. Tape a sheet of paper with various colors on it on the floor. Have children stand back and toss a beanbag. If the beanbag lands on a color, have the child name the color. You can vary the game according to age level.

"I See" Color Game

Tell children that you see something in the room that is a certain color. Let children guess what you see. Then let them take turns saying "I see" as others guess. (Examples: I see something blue that is by the door. Or, I see something purple that someone is wearing.)

Color Tag

Have half the children line up on one side of the room and the other half on the opposite side. Choose one child to be the "painter." The "painter" will call out a color. All children wearing that color try to run across the room without being tagged by the "painter." If a child is tagged, he or she becomes the "painter" and calls out a color, and the game continues.

What Makes a Rainbow?

When the sunlight is separated into its colors by many thousands of raindrops, you will see a rainbow (if the sun is shining behind you and there is rain ahead of you). When a ray of light strikes a raindrop, the light bends. It then separates into its different colors: red, orange, yellow, green, blue, indigo and violet. Together the colors form a curved band. The higher the sun is in the sky, the lower the rainbow will be. A rainbow is best seen when the sun is low in the sky.

Color Scavenger Hunt

Have small groups of children look through old magazines and catalogs to find pictures that have certain colors. Have them cut out the pictures that correspond to the criteria named below. Glue the pictures to a sheet of construction paper. Let each group share their color collage.

- Look for something yellow.
- Look for something with three colors.
- Look for something black.
- Look for something red that you can eat.
- Look for something green that you can wear.
- Look for something blue that can be seen outside.
- Look for an orange letter.

Color Science

In a square glass cake pan, add $1 1/2$ cups milk and 3 tablespoons vegetable oil. (Vary proportions for different effects.) Do not stir. What happens when single drops of liquid food coloring are added over the milk-and-oil mixture? Don't forget to use primary colors only!

Color Exploration

Children have favorite colors from early in life. Just watch them as they color, mark and draw. Lay out various colors, and they'll choose.

- There are many ways to introduce color to children. Begin by taking a walk outside. Write down the colors children see as they call them out. Carry along a box of crayons and let children pick out the color that best matches a color in nature. After your walk, go back to your room and ask children to take a look around. What colors do they see? What colors of clothing are children wearing?

- Give children the opportunity to begin intentionally experiencing colors. Set out two or more paint colors in separate cups. Use an easel, tabletop or floor. Children will love mixing the colors on paper—it's like magic to them.

- Tape a large sheet of paper on a tabletop. Drop dollops of paint of a single, primary color on the paper and encourage children to move the color across the paper with their fingers. Turn on some playful music, classical or sing-along, and let children sing and move around the table as they are painting. Next, splatter a second primary color over the paper. Talk it out, using color language. Even young children will pick it up and begin to understand what you're talking about. "Look at this! What primary color is this?" They answer, "Red!" "Now let's add a second primary color. What is it?" "Blue!" "When we mix them, we get a secondary color. What is it?" "Purple!"

- Let each child choose two colors of primary paint. Place the two colors in a plastic zip-type bag. Make sure the bags are sealed tightly before giving them to children. Have children squeeze the bags. They will be delighted to see a secondary color appear. Use masking tape to hang the new color shades on the windows, or hang them on a clothesline stretched in front of a window so the light can shine through them.

Color Wheels

For this activity you'll need: paint in primary colors, paper plates, colored markers and paper towels for wiping fingers. Cover a work table with white paper. This paper will be part of the experiment and can be used later on as a bulletin board titled "Look What We Can Do Using Red, Yellow and Blue!"

At the table, work with three or four children at a time. Put dollops of red, blue and yellow paint on one paper plate for all to reach. Give each child a paper plate, and have the child print his or her name on the base of the plate. Then put the markers away and flip the plate over. Talk through the process of putting a finger smudge of red paint at one edge of the plate. An inch or so away, each child should add a finger smudge of yellow with a clean finger. Then, in between the two colors, smudge red (from the red finger) and yellow (from the other finger) to make an orange smudge. Continue this process until each child has made a complete seven-color spectrum on his or her "wheel." You should see red, orange, yellow, green, blue, indigo and violet. (For very young children, draw pie-piece lines onto the plate. Smudge one color per pie piece.)

Just for fun, have children add random smudges to the table covering as they go along. You'll have an amazing variety of color mixes when you've finished. Celebrate these colors. Turn on happy music and let children dance while waving colored crepe-paper streamers.

Chromatography

Chromatography is the process of separating colors into distinct bands or spots by permitting a solution to flow through an absorbent material. This is not nearly as complicated as it sounds.

1. Buy a yard of stretch, cotton fabric and cut it into five-inch squares. Pour hydrogen peroxide into a pie tin or other low-sided container. You will also need medicine droppers; rubber bands; clear plastic cups; and red, yellow and blue markers. Cover each child's work space with newspaper.

2. Each child will "dot" a fabric square using the primary-colored markers. Next, they will lay the dotted fabric square over a plastic cup and secure it with a rubber band. Have children fill a medicine dropper with peroxide and squeeze it over the marker dots on the fabric square. What happens will amaze everyone!

3. Allow the finished product sufficient drying time, then mount the squares on colored construction paper for display. Ask each child to write his or her name and the word *chromatography* on the mounting paper.

Bulletin Board

Colors

If you introduce St. Patrick's Day as part of your curriculum, you might want to reinforce color recognition with this playful bulletin board. Using the pattern on page 33, cut out paper paint cans. Tip these "cans" in varying angles across the bulletin board, and add paint drips from the tops as if paint is spilling from the cans. Title the paint cans with the following rainbow colors: Top o' the Arc Red, Irish Orange, Leprechaun Lemon, Shamrock Shine, Not True Blarney Blue, In-Ye'-Go Indigo (add a leprechaun jumping into this paint can) and Violet's Jig.

Pattern for Bulletin Board

Books — Colors

Color Your World with Books!

The Color Kittens
by Margaret Wise Brown, Golden Books, 2000

The Great Blueness and Other Predicaments
by Arnold Lobel, Harper & Row, 1968

Hailstones and Halibut Bones: Adventures in Color
by Mary O'Neill and John Wallner (Illustrator), Doubleday, 1990

Kipper's Book of Colors
by Mick Inkpen, Harcourt, 1995

Over the Rainbow!
by Barbara Taylor, Random House, 1992

Planting a Rainbow
by Lois Ehlert, Harcourt Brace Jovanovich, 1988

Rainbow Crow
retold by Nancy Van Laan, Knopf, 1989

The Rainbow Fish
by Marcus Pfister, North-South Books, 1992

Raindrops and Rainbows
by Rose Wyler, Julian Messner, 1989

Sparky's Rainbow Repair
by Max Haynes; Lothrop, Lee & Shepard; 1992

Crafts   Colors

Rubbings

Have children bring flat items to class: leaves, books with raised titles, pennies, corrugated cardboard, lace, plastic net bags and so on. Each child will need a 4" x 4" piece of white paper. Place the paper over the objects, then show children how to rub the side of a dark-colored crayon over the paper until outlines and textures appear. Have children frame their rubbings by gluing them on larger squares of colorful construction paper.

Rainbow Bubbles

Make or buy bubble solution. Have children make pipe-cleaner wands, bending one end of a pipe cleaner in a circle. Let them dip their wands in the bubble solution and hold them up. As they watch the soap bubble film on the wand, what colors do they see? Do the colors change?

Mixing Colors

Invite children to experiment with colors. Using the butterfly pattern on page 36, have children paint each side of the butterfly. While the paint is still wet, have them fold the butterfly in half. What color is the butterfly now?

Rainbow Sticks

Each child will need: large paper towel tube, 2 rubber bands, 1 sheet of white paper, glue, markers, uncooked rice, 6 to 7 pieces of 4" x 4" newspaper print, 1 sheet of construction paper and tape.

Have children spread glue around the outside of one end of the tube. Place a piece of white paper over the end and cover it, securing it with the rubber band. Show children how to loosely crumple the pieces of newspaper and put them in the tube, along with about ½ cup of rice. Glue a cover on the open end of the tube. (Remove the rubber bands when the ends have dried.)

Have children draw a rainbow on the sheet of construction paper. Wrap this around the tube and secure it with tape. As children slowly turn the tube over, it will sound like rain. Shaking the tube will make it sound like maracas.

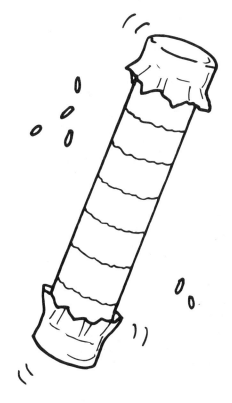

"Mixing Colors" Pattern

Poems

Colors

Colors Action Rhyme

Personal Colors

Children will enjoy singing this song and doing the actions when their personal colors are mentioned. They may need to be reminded to only do the actions when it is their turn. You may want to add other verses dealing with the colors of children's clothing, shoes, houses and so on.

To the tune of "If You're Happy and You Know It"

If your eyes are blue, clap your hands.
If your eyes are blue, clap your hands.
If your eyes are blue, show us just what you can do.
If your eyes are blue, clap your hands.

If your eyes are brown, clap your hands.
If your eyes are brown, clap your hands.
If your eyes are brown, show us just what you can do.
If your eyes are brown, clap your hands.

If your eyes are green, clap your hands.
If your eyes are green, clap your hands.
If your eyes are green, show us just what you can do.
If your eyes are green, clap your hands.

If your hair is brown, clap your hands.
If your hair is brown, clap your hands.
If your hair is brown, show us just what you can do.
If your hair is brown, clap your hands.

If your hair is blonde, clap your hands.
If your hair is blonde, clap your hands.
If your hair is blonde, show us just what you can do.
If your hair is blonde, clap your hands.

If your hair is black, clap your hands.
If your hair is black, clap your hands.
If your hair is black, show us just what you can do.
If your hair is black, clap your hands.

If your hair is red, clap your hands.
If your hair is red, clap your hands.
If your hair is red, show us just what you can do.
If your hair is red, clap your hands.

by Mary Tucker

Colors Action Rhyme

A Colorful Year

As you read the poem, hold up the colors mentioned. Let children choose their favorites.

If you could color each month of the year,
What would you choose? Do you know?
Well, January would have to be white
Because of all that snow.
February might be pink
For valentines given away.
March would need to be green, of course,
Because of St. Patrick's Day.
April would be light blue, I guess,
Because of all those showers,
And May could be bright purple—
The color of so many flowers.
Since June begins the summer,
It should be yellow, I'd say.
July would have to be red, white and blue
For Independence Day.
August should be gold, I think,
For those golden days in the sun.
September would be reddish-brown
For fall has just begun.
October would be orange
For pumpkins ripening fast.
November would be brown because,
The green grass never lasts!
December would be red and green,
Like holiday decorations.
And all these colorful months combined
Make a year-long color sensation!

by Mary Tucker

Snacks

Colors

⚠ Make sure you are aware of any food allergies or restrictions children may have. Be sure children wash their hands, and fruits and vegetables before they eat.

Rainbow Toast

For this snack, you'll need: paper plates, small containers, 3/4 cup milk, liquid food coloring, new watercolor brushes, white bread slices, a toaster oven and colored sugar crystals (cake decorations).

Have each child write his or her name on the edge of a paper plate. Mix milk and food coloring in the small containers to use as "paint." Make as many colors of the rainbow as you can. Place a slice of bread on each plate and have children paint "rainbows" by dipping their brushes in the colored milk. Sprinkle the colored sugar on the rainbows while they are still wet. Toast, cool and enjoy!

Tasting Colors

Consider the natural colors in the foods we eat. Lay out a beautiful rainbow of fruit. Depending on the season, use strawberries, cherries, watermelon, red apples, orange wedges, yellow apples, banana slices, green grapes, blueberries, plums and purple grapes. Try the same thing using fresh vegetables such as radishes, carrots, squash, sweet peas, beans and eggplant. Allow children to explore the eggplant and other colorful food items. Using plastic knives and fingers, they can look for seeds or color changes between the insides and the skins. Then let children taste each fruit or vegetable. Does it taste like its color? What should red taste like?

Make Rainbow Gelatin

Using different colors of gelatin, make layers of color, one on top of another. Follow package directions, and let each layer set before adding another.

Faster version: Make several colors of gelatin, in separate pans, according to the directions. Let set and cut each color in small squares. Have each child put several different colors in a cup. Top with whipped topping.

39

TLC10527 Copyright © Teaching & Learning Company, Carthage, IL 62321-0010

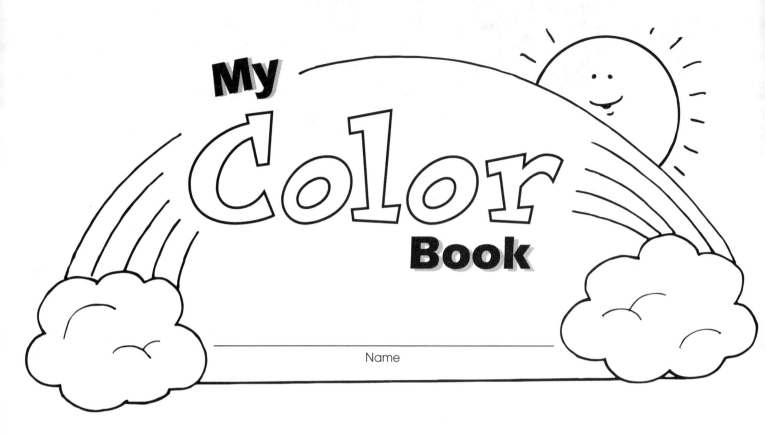

Name

I can draw three things that are red.

I know my primary colors. I can color the crayons.

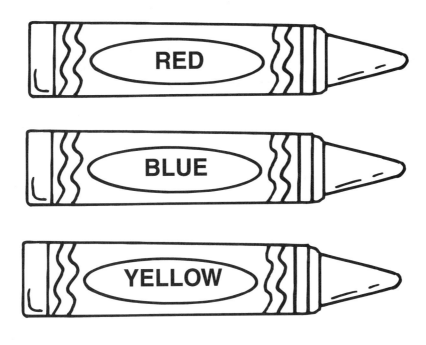

2

Here are three secondary colors. I can color the crayons.

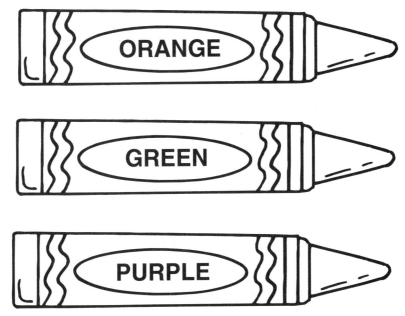

3

41

I can write the names of six colors.

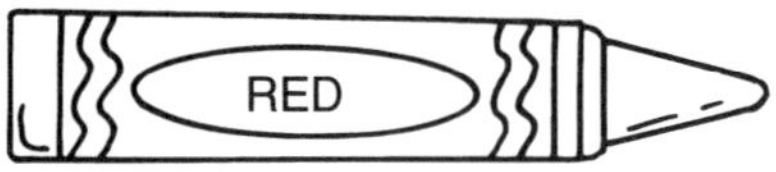

RED   BLUE   YELLOW

When we mix blue and yellow, we get

GREEN

When we mix red and yellow, we get

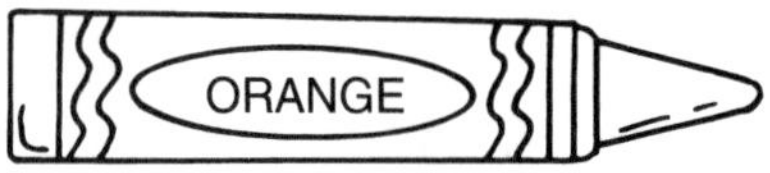

ORANGE

When we mix red and white, we get

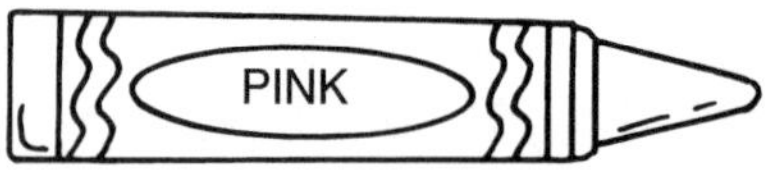

PINK

When we mix black and white, we get

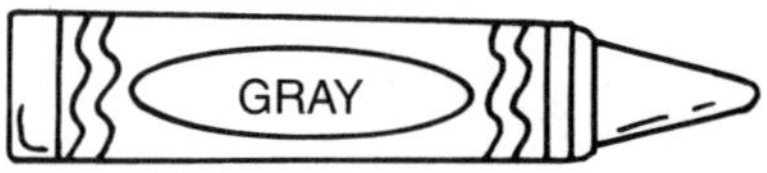

GRAY

Fruits and vegetables come in lots of different colors.

Peas are _____

Bananas are _____

Carrots are _____

A tomato is _____

My favorite blue thing is _____

My favorite fruit is _____

My favorite animal is _____

My favorite color is _____

The color of my favorite flower is _____

The color of my favorite food is _____

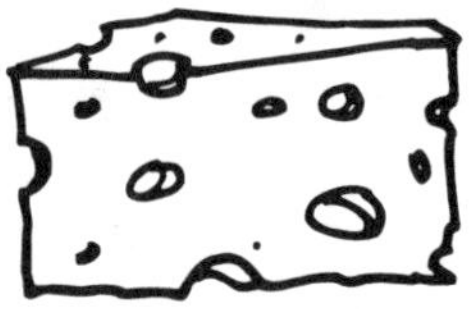

My hair color is _____

My eyes are _____

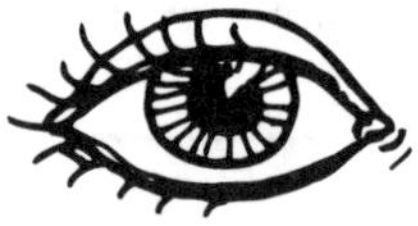

My skin is _____

Name

Rainbow Colors

Color the picture.

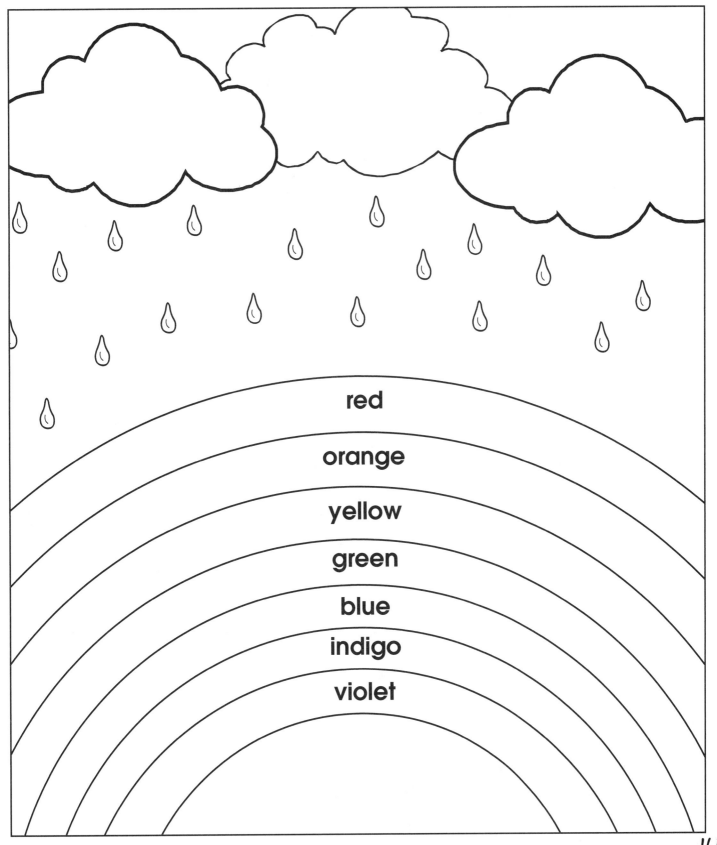

red

orange

yellow

green

blue

indigo

violet

Name

Gumball Fun

Color 6 gumballs red.
Color 2 gumballs orange.
Color 1 gumball yellow.
Color 4 gumballs green.
Color 3 gumballs blue.
Color 5 gumballs purple.

Color Recognition

Draw a line from the picture to its color.

green

pink

red

brown

black

gray

purple

blue

Name

Color the Pictures

red   **blue**   **orange**

brown   **yellow**   **green**

Animal Lineup

Follow the directions.

Color the second frog red. Color the first frog blue.
Color the sixth frog green. Color the fifth frog yellow.

Color the seventh ladybug red. Color the sixth ladybug pink.
Color the first ladybug blue. Color the fifth ladybug green.

Color the third worm green. Color the first worm yellow.
Color the fourth worm red. Color the fifth worm orange.

Color the second turtle pink. Color the first turtle orange.
Color the sixth turtle purple. Color the fifth turtle green.

Name

✂✂✂✂✂ Clip Art ✂✂✂✂✂

Use this art as a page topper for stories, poems and so on.

Activities

Numbers

Counting Fun
Use a marker to number the cups of an egg carton from 1 to 12. Have children put one object (bean, candy or cereal) in the cup marked *1* and continue filling each cup with the correct number of items.

Count by 10s
Each child will need a long piece of yarn (12"-18") and some colored O-shaped cereal. Have children count out 10 of each color and string them on their pieces of yarn. Count by 10s.

Pet Shop
Invite children to bring a stuffed animal from home. Price each animal from $1 to $10. Provide children with play money. Have them buy one or two pets. Encourage children to take turns being customers and storekeepers.

Cookie Math
Cut 24 circle shapes from light brown paper to make cookies. On half of the cookies, write the numbers 1 to 12. On the others, draw 1 to 12 chocolate chips. Place the cookies in a jar. Invite children to match each pair of cookies.

Weekly Guessing
Every week fill a clean jar with individually wrapped candies. During the week, let children look at the jar. At the end of the week have them guess how many candies are in the jar. Record their guesses. Then open the jar and help children count the candies. Help children divide the candies evenly. Use this activity to practice counting by 2s, 5s and 10s.

53

Building Blocks

Use blocks to build a tower. Have children count how many blocks it took to build it.

Number Lineup

Prepare a set of cards numbered from 1 to the number of children in your class. Mix the cards up, and give one to each child. Have children arrange themselves in numerical order from lowest to highest. You can also practice simple addition problems such as, "We have 3 apples and 2 bananas. How many pieces of fruit do we have?" The child with the 5 on his or her card would then step forward.

Button, Button

Have children sort buttons by specific attributes (size, color, number of holes and so on). Then have children count the groups and record them.

Domino Math

This is a fun way to practice basic math facts. Have each child use dominoes to write math fact family sentences. For example, if a domino has three dots and two dots on it, the child would write *3 + 2 =* and then write the answer.

Go Fish!

Make several fish shapes of various colors (See patterns on page 55.). Write simple addition problems or glue different numbers of sequins (for scales) on each fish. Then put the fish in a fishbowl. Each child pulls a fish out of the bowl and answers the addition problem or says how many scales the fish has.

"Go Fish!" Patterns

55

Bulletin Board

Numbers

1. Cover the bulletin board with red paper. Cut letters for the caption from black paper, and put them across the top of the board.

2. Have children use markers or crayons to write numbers all over the background paper.

3. Display each child's school picture on the board.

4. Work with children to figure out how many people there are in various categories, as shown above or come up with your own sorting criteria.

5. Print the statistics on colored construction paper strips and attach to the board.

Books — Numbers

Books You Can Count On!

Animal Numbers
by Bert Kitchen, Dial, 1987

Fish Eyes: A Book You Can Count On
by Lois Ehlert, Harcourt Brace, 2001

The Icky Bug Counting Book
by Jerry Pallotta, Charlesbridge, 1992

Inch by inch
by Leo Lionni, Astro-Honor, 1960

Kipper's Book of Numbers
by Mick Inkpen, Harcourt, 1995

Mouse Count
by Ellen Stoll Walsh, Voyager Picture Books, 1995

One Hundred Hungry Ants
by Elinor J. Pinczes, Scholastic, 1993

One More and One Less
by Giulio Maestro, Crown, 1974

Snappy Little Numbers
by Kate Lee, Millbrook, 1998

Witzy's Numbers
by Suzy Spafford, Cartwheel Books, 2002

Crafts

Numbers

Popcorn Math

Copy the popcorn shape below. Have each child cut 12 popcorn shapes. Have children write a number from 1 to 9 on each shape. On the remaining 3 popcorn shapes, have them make a minus, plus and equal sign. Use the paper popcorn pieces to make number sentences. Children can use real popcorn pieces to show the answer.

Number Soup

Have children number off from 1 to 12. After 12, have them start over until every child has a number. Tell them you're going to let them decide what ingredients to put in an imaginary pot of soup. Let each child suggest what ingredient he or she will contribute. (For example: 1 chicken, 2 potatoes, 3 carrots, etc.) Have children color their ingredients, write the numbers on them and then cut them out. Put all the ingredients in a pan and pretend to stir them together. Patterns provided on page 59.

Popcorn Sacks

Give each child a white paper lunch sack. Have them use red markers to draw lines up and down the sacks. Then use zigzag scissors to cut 1" off the top of the sacks. Fill sacks with popcorn. Have children do simple addition problems using popcorn pieces. They can also use the pieces to count by 2s and so on.

Paper Chains

Use a paper cutter to cut colored paper strips. Give each child 12 strips. Have children write a number from 1 to 12 on each strip, and then mix them up. Children make paper chains, putting the loops in numerical order.

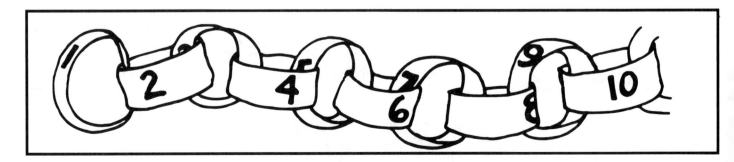

"Number Soup" Patterns

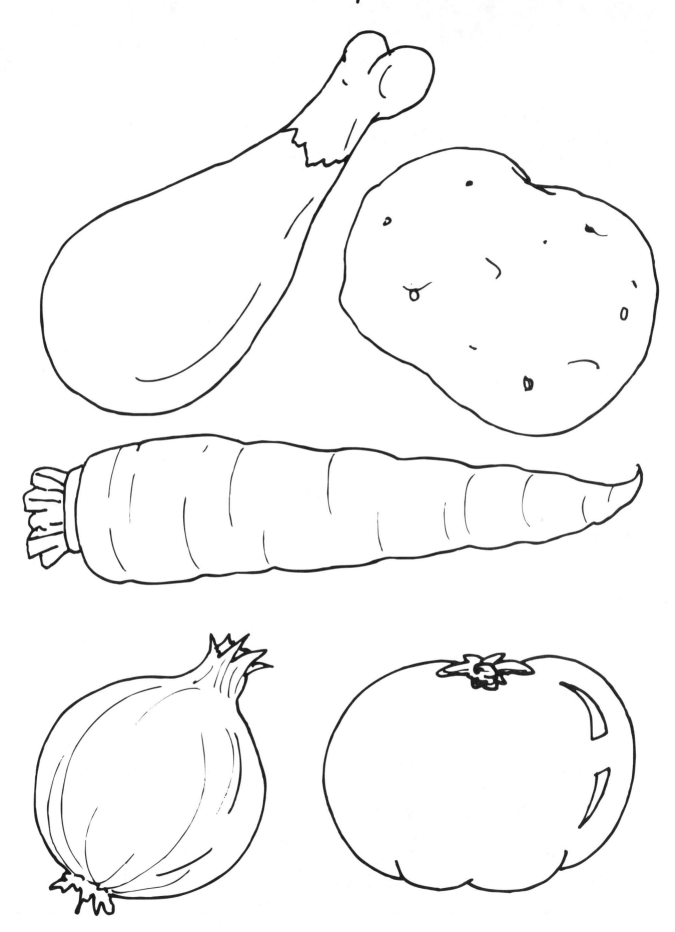

Poems

Numbers

Number Fun ACTION RHYME

Numbers Exercise

Demonstrate each exercise in the rhyme to make sure children understand how to do all of them. Then as you say the rhyme together, they may do the correct number of exercises. Make sure you have plenty of room so children don't bump into one another.

1 big jump as high as I can go.
2 giant steps going very, very slow,
3 body twirls make me kind of dizzy.
4 hops on one leg have me in a tizzy!
5 bend-overs to lightly touch the floor.
6 steps backward—not one step more.
7 baby steps; I hardly move at all.
8 knee bends with my hands against the wall.
9 leg kicks up very, very high.
10 flaps of my arms—I can almost fly!
11 jumping jacks. Now I'm almost done.
12 claps with my hands. Exercise is fun!

by Mary Tucker

Number Fun ACTION RHYME

A Counting Fingerplay

Before teaching this rhyme to children, cut 12 nut shapes from brown paper and put them on a wall or bulletin board. Count them before and after the fingerplay. If you can find a squirrel cut-out to put among the nuts, it will make the activity more fun.

Little Sammy Squirrel ran up and down his tree,
   (Run fingers up and down one arm.)
Carrying nuts to hide them secretly.
   (Hold out hands as if holding nuts.)
The first nut he dropped into a hole he had found.
   (Make a hole with one hand and poke a finger from the other hand into it.)
He put the second nut under a leaf on the ground.
   (Cup one hand over the other one.)
The third nut he hid in an old flowerpot.
   (Hold hands in the shape of a flowerpot.)
He put the fourth nut in a tree he liked a lot.
   (Shake outstretched arms like tree limbs.)
He hid the fifth nut underneath the tool shed.
   (Kneel down and point down low.)
The sixth nut he buried in a lovely flower bed.
   (Pretend to dig with hands.)
The seventh nut he hid inside an old boot.
   (Point to your foot.)
The eighth nut went into a box that held fruit.
   (Rub your stomach and lick your lips.)
He stashed away the ninth nut in a pile of rocks.
   (Stack closed fists on top of one another like a pile of rocks.)
The tenth nut he hid underneath an old box.
   (Draw a square shape with fingers.)
He put the eleventh nut in an empty brown sack.
   (Hold one hand flat and pretend to drop a nut into it with the other hand.)
Then he ate the twelfth nut for a little snack.
   (Pretend to eat a nut like a squirrel.)
Now all Sammy's nuts are hidden away.
   (Shade eyes with hand as if searching.)
Will he ever find them when he looks for them someday?
   (Shrug shoulders and raise hands as if asking a question.)
by Mary Tucker

Snacks

Numbers

Pepperoni Pizza

Follow the directions from a pizza mix to make enough pizza for every child to have some. Have children add pepperoni slices on top of the unbaked pizza. Bake according to directions. Cut pizza into slices. Have children count how many pepperoni pieces they have on each slice.

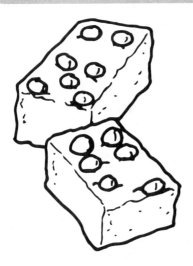

Domino Brownies

Make brownies according to the box directions. Let cool and cut into rectangular shapes. Give each child several m & m's™ to place on top of the brownies (like dominoes).

Giant Cookie

Make your favorite sugar or chocolate chip cookie recipe, or buy ready-made dough. Press dough into a large round pizza pan and bake. When cooled, let children frost the cookie. Then decorate it with 10 each of 10 different candies to make 100 (chocolate chips, white chocolate chips, sprinkles, jelly beans, Skittles™, Reese's Pieces™, candy corn, red hots and other small candies).

⚠ Make sure you are aware of any food allergies or restrictions children may have. Be sure children wash their hands before they eat.

My Numbers Book

Numbers on the loose with Mother Goose!

_____
Name

1, 2
Buckle my shoe.

3, 4
Knock at the door.

5, 6
Pick up sticks.

7, 8
Lay them straight.

9, 10
A big fat hen.

11, 12
I can count by myself!

What is your favorite number?

Draw that many shapes.

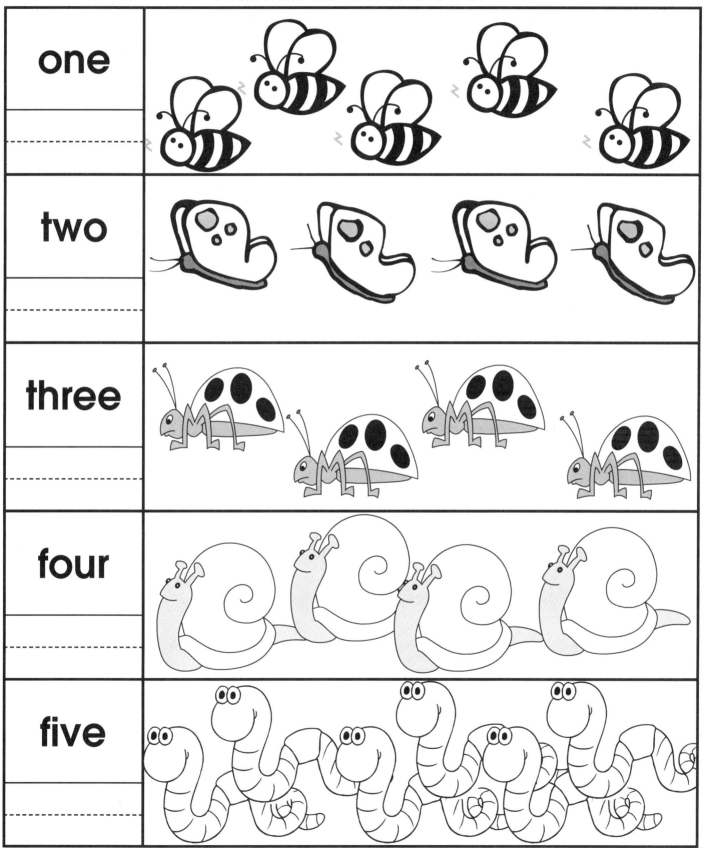

Name

Addition Practice
Use the number line to help you find the sums.

```
   5        1        2        4
  +2       +3       +1       +3
  ---      ---      ---      ---

   4        5        7        5
  +4       +1       +3       +5
  ---      ---      ---      ---

   6        8        3        4
  +2       +1       +3       +5
  ---      ---      ---      ---
```

What Is Missing?

Look at each set of blocks.
What number comes in between?
Write the number.

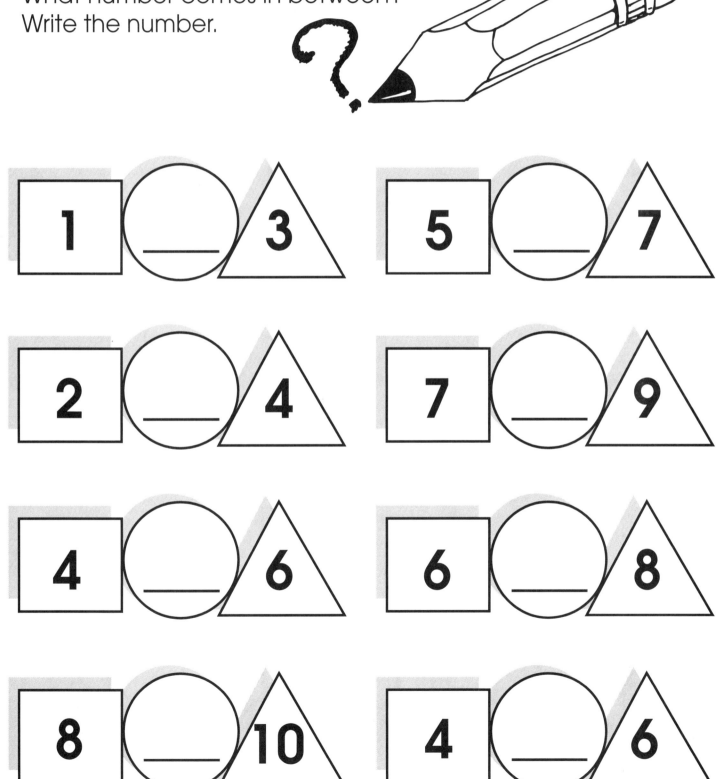

Name

Count the Gumballs

Use the gumballs to help you add the numbers.
Write each sum in the box.

3 ○○○
+ 2 ○○

1 ○
+ 1 ○

2 ○○
+ 2 ○○

3 ○○○
+ 3 ○○○

2 ○○
+ 5 ○○○ ○○

4 ○○○○
+ 4 ○○○○

1 ○
+ 4 ○○○○

8 ○○○○ ○○○○
+ 2 ○○

6 ○○○ ○○○
+ 4 ○○○○

7 ○○○○ ○○○
+ 1 ○

70

Animal Lineup

Color two frogs green.
Color one frog blue.

Color one frog red.
Color two frogs purple.

Circle the third ladybug red.
Color the first ladybug orange.

Cross out the fourth ladybug.
Color the fifth ladybug blue.

Color the third worm green.
Color the fourth worm brown.

Color the first worm red.
Color the fifth worm orange.

Color three turtles green.
Color two turtles yellow.

Color one turtle blue.

Name

Follow the Numbers Maze

Follow the numbers in the correct order to get through the maze.

Name _____

My Numbers Page

Clip Art

Activities — Shapes

Show-n-Tell Shapes

Have the following items and others you choose available to show children: penny, towel, picture of the sun, pillowcase, book, picture of the moon, dollar bill, quarter, stamp, envelope, sheet of paper, brick, door, cookie, top of a drinking glass, plate, postcard, ball, CD, bottom of a glass. Ask children to identify the shape of each.

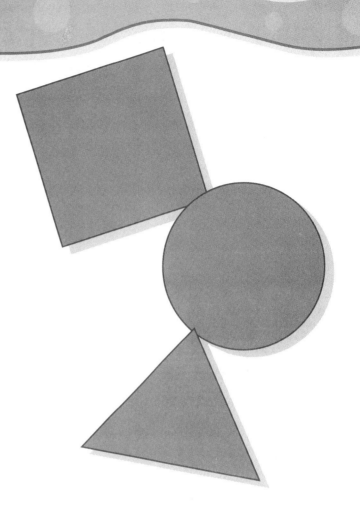

Shape Think

This is a good game to play when children have mastered their shapes. Give children a box of shapes. Let them choose a shape without looking. Then ask them, "What kind of object can you think of that looks like the shape you are holding?"

Shape Drawings

Make copies of the shapes on page 95. Ask children to trace the shapes and then color them. After cutting out each shape, children should put their shapes together to form a picture.

Foam Shapes

Draw shapes on sheets of craft foam, one sheet for each child. Have children cut the thin sheet of foam into their own shapes. Ask each child to decorate a tissue box to use for storage. Then they can put their foam shapes in the box.

Shape Guess

Number various shapes. Ask a child to pick a number from 1 to 10. Then the child has to name the shape that corresponds to the number they chose. If number 1 is a triangle, say, "What shape is it, can you guess?"

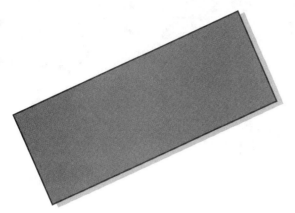

Make a Pattern

Place laminated shapes on a table (made from template shapes). Make certain you have reproduced plenty of shapes. Place several shapes, one after the other, in a pattern. Ask children what shape comes next. Make several different patterns so each child can have a turn. Ask individual children to make a pattern and have their classmates figure out what comes next.

Shape Holder

Materials
- construction paper
- glue or stapler
- crayons
- tracing shapes
- pencil
- colored poster board
- scissors
- decorative stickers

Directions

1. Fold a sheet of construction paper one-third of the way up. Crease the fold. Glue or staple the sides to form a pocket.

2. Ask children to label the paper with their name and to write *My Shapes* above the pocket. Children can then decorate their shape holders with stickers.

3. Provide plastic or cardboard templates for children to use to cut their own set of shapes from colored poster board. (Shapes patterns found on page 95.)

4. Have children store their shape collections in their decorated shape holders.

"I Spy" Shapes

Play this popular game using shapes! Look around the room and make up clues for objects that are shapes. "I spy something that is round like a circle." "I spy something white that is a square." Give clues appropriate to the age of the children. After they are familiar with the game, let each child have a turn "I Spying."

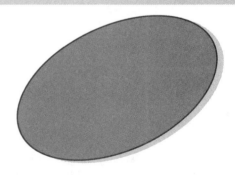

Printmaking with Sponges

Cut triangles, squares and other shapes from sponges. Give each child a sheet of paper and a few sponge shapes. Ask them to paint their sponges with watercolors or tempera paint. Then have children press the shapes onto their papers to make a collage of shapes.

Bulletin Board

Shapes

Happy Shape Face

1. Enlarge the pattern on page 78, or draw your own face. Place the face on a bulletin board.

2. Print *Happy Shape Face* at the top of the bulletin board, or cut letters from colored paper and put them up.

3. Each week, cut out one shape from colored paper.

4. Tape the shape where the "nose" should be on the Happy Shape Face. Ask children, "What shape is the Happy Shape Face's nose today?"

5. Ask children to think of shapes around the room that look like the shape on the bulletin board.

6. During the week, have children cut pictures from magazines that are similar to the shape on the bulletin board. Glue the pictures around the Happy Shape Face.

7. Repeat this the following week with another shape.

Happy Shape Face Pattern

Books

I Spy Shapes in Art
by Lucy Micklethwait, Greenwillow, 2004

Let's Draw a Bear with Squares
by Kathy Campbell, Power Kids Press, 2004

Mouse Shapes
by Ellen Stoll Walsh, Harcourt, 2007

Museum Shapes
by The Metropolitan Museum of Art, Little Brown, 2005

The Shape of Things
by Dayle Anne Dodds, Candlewick, 1996

Shapes, Shapes, Shapes
by Tana Hoban, HarperTrophy, 1996

So Many Circles, So Many Squares
by Tana Hoban, Greenwillow, 1998

When a Line Bends . . . A Shape Begins
by Rhonda Gowler Greene, Houghton Mifflin, 2001

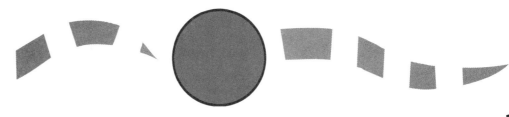

Crafts

Shapes

Monarch Butterfly

Give children practice with shapes by having them complete these simple craft projects. After making the butterfly and ladybug, let children use brightly colored foam sheets to create their own bugs or other animals.

Materials
- black foam
- orange foam
- yellow foam
- scissors
- glue
- gray or green foam
- string
- wiggle eyes (optional)
- pipe cleaners (optional)

Directions
1. Cut out the shapes below to use as patterns.
2. Cut one butterfly from black foam.
3. Cut out the gray wing patterns from orange foam.
4. Cut the rest of the wing patterns from yellow foam. Glue all in place as shown.
5. Cut one body from gray or green foam and glue in place. Attach string on back and hang.
6. Optional: Add wiggle eyes and pipe-cleaner antennas.

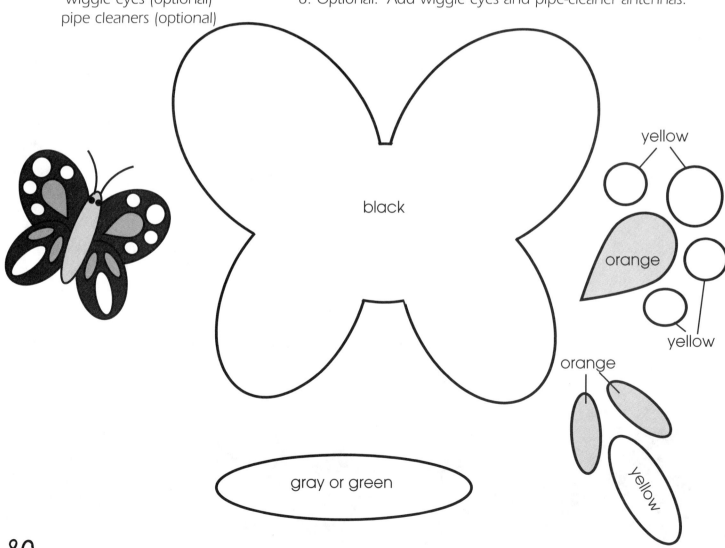

Ladybug

Materials
red foam
black foam
scissors
glue
wiggle eyes

Directions
1. Cut one body from red foam.
2. Cut one head from black foam. Glue head to back of body.
3. Cut six legs from black foam. Glue legs to back of body.
4. Cut several spots from black foam (or use markers to decorate). Glue spots to top of body.
5. Glue two wiggle eyes to the head.

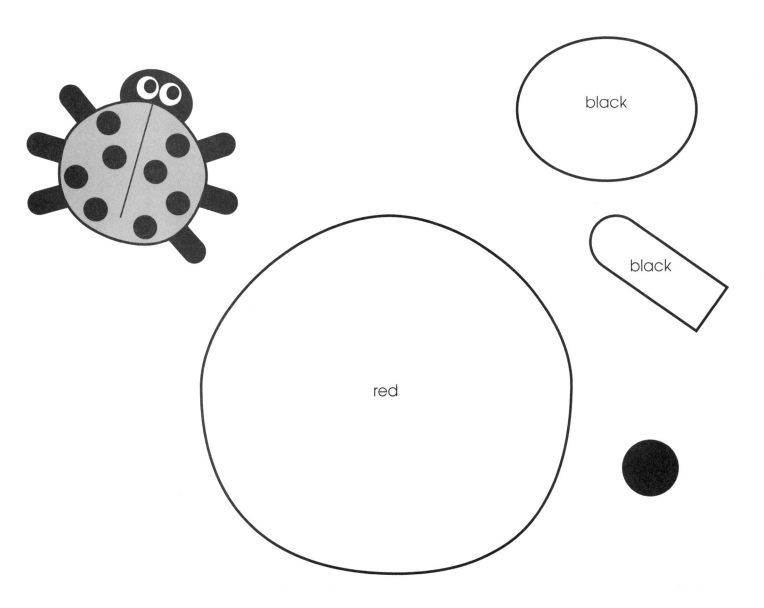

Poems

Shapes

Shapes ACTION RHYME

*As children are saying the rhyme,
show them the shapes mentioned in the poem.*

There are lots of shapes around the room—
(Point around room.)
So many to be found!
Let's look to see what we can find,
Without making a sound.
(Place finger to lips.)

I can see a triangle.
(Outline the triangle with finger.)
It looks like a piece of pie.
(Rub tummy.)

There's an oval over there.
(Outline an oval with finger.)
It looks like an egg to fry!
(Pretend to fry egg.)

I can see a square,
(Outline square with finger.)
Like a window to outside fun.
(Point at window.)

And look, there's a circle
(Outline circle shape.)
That looks just like the bright round sun!
(Point at sun.)

What about the rectangle
(Outline rectangle.)
That's hiding under there?
(Point.)
It reminds me of a book
(Outline book.)
That I'd like to read and share!
(Hold up a book about shapes and then read it to the class.)

Shapes SONGS

If You Have This Shape

To the tune of "If You're Happy and You Know It"

Give each child a set of shapes made from cardboard or paper.

If you have this shape and know it, find a square!
If you have this shape and know it, find a square!
If you have a square and know it, then you really ought to show it.
If you have this shape and know it, find a square.

Other Verses

If you have this shape and know it, find an oval.
 . . . a triangle.
 . . . a circle.
 . . . a rectangle, etc.

Draw, Draw, Draw This Shape

To the tune of "Row Your Boat"

Draw, draw, draw this shape, carefully this way.
You have done it very well! Shapes are fun today!

As you sing each verse, draw the shape you are singing about on the chalkboard or chart paper while children draw their own on smaller sheets of paper.

A Shape Poem

I just learned my shapes today:

Triangle, square and circle. Hooray!

One shape looks like a pizza slice.

One looks like a slice of bread.

The other looks just like the sun . . .

Or maybe a ball instead.

I used these shapes to make a picture.

See how I made the tree?

Here's my cozy little house,

My puppy dog

And me!

Snacks

Shapes

Spaghetti Shapes

Prepare pasta according to directions on the box. Place cooked spaghetti in a bowl. Let cool. Give each child a paper plate and one or two strands of spaghetti. Have children use the spaghetti to make shapes on their plates.

Cheese and Crackers Snack Shapes

Use a cookie cutter to cut cheese slices into circles; use a knife to cut them into squares. Alternate the cheese slices with round and square crackers on a plate. As children enjoy this snack, ask them what shape they are eating.

S'mores

Don't forget the ever-popular s'mores when studying shapes. You'll have square graham crackers, rectangular pieces of chocolate and cylindrical marshmallows that get flattened into circles or ovals!

Orange Slice Shapes

Choosing which shapes to make and eat makes this a fun snack. Help children peel oranges. Place the separated segments on a paper plate. Ask children what kind of shape they would like to create from the slices. Or say, "Can you make a triangle or a square on your plate?" Arrange the orange slices to form the shape. After children are done making shapes, it's time to eat!

Triangle Gelatin

Make gelatin according to package directions. Pour into triangle molds (found in any kitchen or craft store). Refrigerate until set. Ask children what shape they are eating. Or use cookie cutters to cut shapes from gelatin made in a flat shallow pan.

_____
Name

triangle

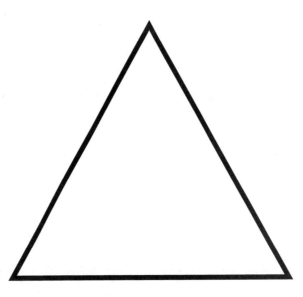

A triangle has three sides. Each side is a straight line.

square

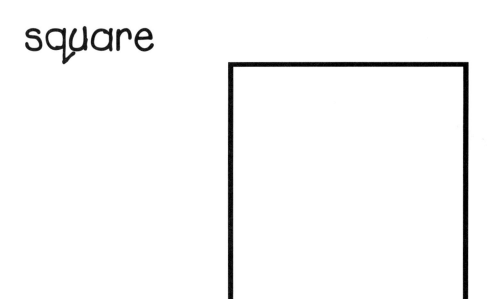

A square has four sides. Each side is the same.

2

---

rectangle

A rectangle has four sides. Two sides are the same.

3

oval

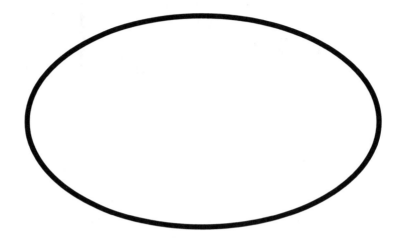

An oval looks like an egg.

---

circle

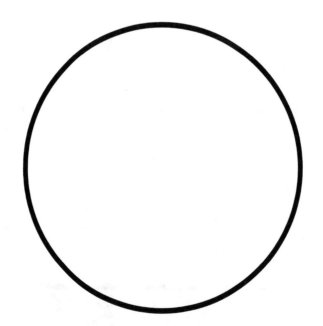

A circle is round like the sun.

star

A star has five points.

6

---

diamond

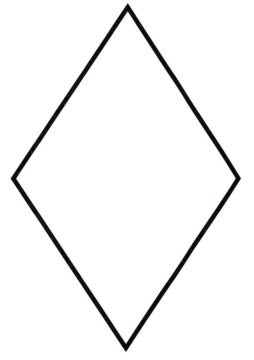

A diamond has four sides and looks like a kite.

7

Color the Shapes

1. Color the triangle green.

2. Color the rectangle red.

3. Color the square blue.

4. Color the circle yellow.

5. Color the oval purple.

6. Color the star orange.

Name _____

Shapes

Draw a ring around the squares.

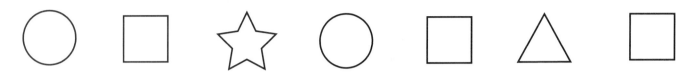

Draw an X in the circle.

Color all the shapes red except for the square.

Color the triangles blue.

Draw a line through the circle.

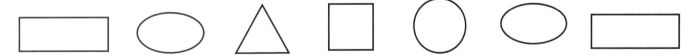

Draw a ring around the rectangles.

TLC10527 Copyright © Teaching & Learning Company, Carthage, IL 62321-0010

Shape Patterns

Find the pattern.
Draw the shape that comes next in each row.

1.

2.

3.

4.

5. ⬡ ⬡ ⬭ ⬡ ⬡ ⬭

6. ⬠ ○ ⬠ ○ ⬠

7. △ ☆ △ ☆ △

Name

The Shape of Me

Make a picture of yourself using shapes.
How many different shapes can you use? Color your picture.

Name _____

My Shape Page

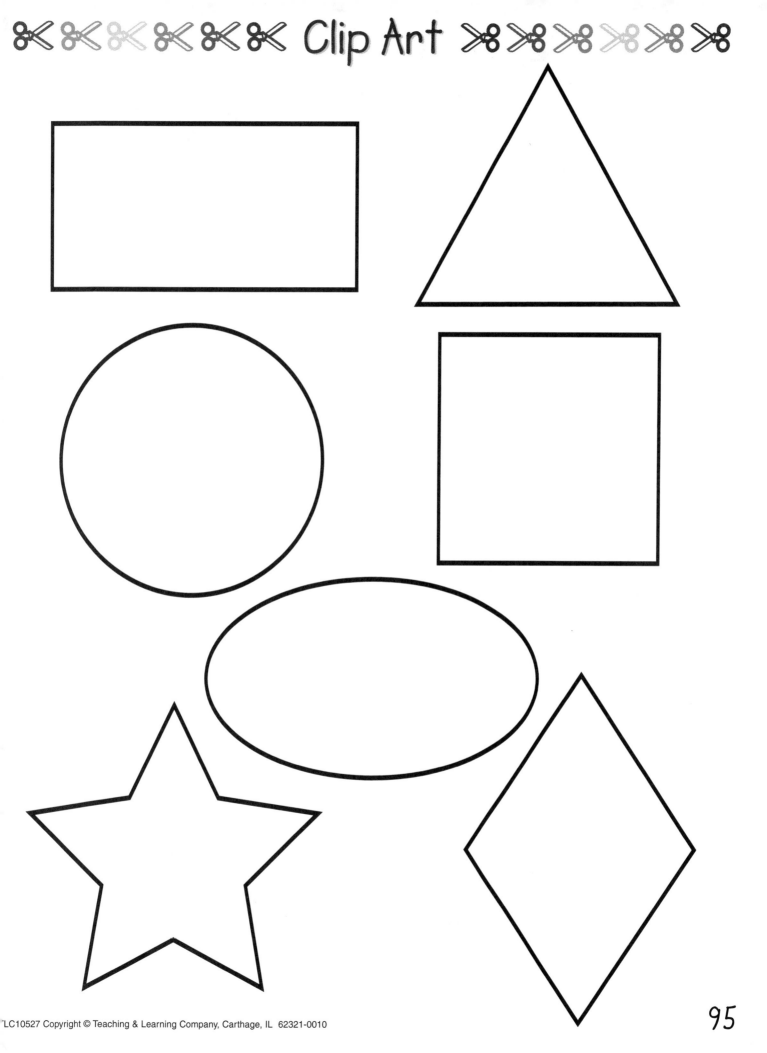